CRIES OF SWIMMERS

UNIVERSITY OF UTAH PRESS POETRY SERIES

MAURA STANTON

CRIES OF SWIMMERS

UNIVERSITY OF UTAH PRESS   SALT LAKE CITY   1984

UNIVERSITY OF UTAH PRESS POETRY SERIES
DAVE SMITH, *Editor*

See ACKNOWLEDGMENTS, page 72, for permission statements.
The author wishes to thank the National Endowment for the Arts
for its support in writing this book.

The paper in this book meets the standards for
permanence and durability established by the
Committee on Production Guidelines for Book Longevity
of the Council on Library Resources.

LIBRARY OF CONGRESS CATALOGING IN PUBLICATION DATA

Stanton, Maura.
    Cries of swimmers.

    (University of Utah Press Poetry Series)
    I. Title.
PS3569.T3337C7   1984   811'.54   84-2227
ISBN 0-87480-232-6

for Richard

CONTENTS

IV

I

AT THE COCHISE TOURIST PAVILION

Yesterday I saw my first mirage
Spreading for acres across a desert basin,
The water blue and flat, reflecting mountains.
The image lasted for miles. Astonished,
I searched my map for explanations,
Some new dam, or reservoir, or flood plain,
But only the black words "Bombing Range"
Crossed that white space beside the highway.
Of course I've seen the highway mirages
Even in the midwest, without sand or cactus,
When suddenly the road ahead turns into water,
Reflecting the slow passage of the clouds
Shaped like the cows and sheep of dozing giants,
Until you blink or traffic breaks the illusion.
Wasn't this an illusion? Shading my eyes
I turned the lovely water into caliche,
That zone of calcium under the parched soil
Blown off by the practiced rake of the bombers.
But then I felt a chill. I could imagine
Some old prospector leaning down to view
The image of his own inverted face
Before he choked on a bright handful of dust,
For my lake reappeared, dotted with sails,
With houses on the far shore under the trees.

At the tourist pavilion, under a glass case,
I found the chart of ancient Lake Cochise
Where strange fish once swam, their starry tails
Imprinted on an occasional rock or cliff face.
The old travelers had seen this same mirage,
Leaning out the windows of the Butterfield stage.
And even Coronado may have crossed the ghost water,
The waves turning to sand around his ankles,
The first of his seven golden cities vanishing.

The air-conditioned air stroked my face
While I stood there, feeling pale and watery
As if from certain angles I might disappear.
I'd been seeing backward (Eight thousand years!)
In a way I hadn't been able to see last summer
Passing under the Lion's Gate at Mycenae
When I strained my eyes, trying to find Helen
Or Agamemnon or the royal children
Buried with gold leaf on hands and feet.
All I discovered then was the roar of jets
Crossing the valley below the grave circle
At sonic speed, so that the tour guide
Shouted her list of treasures, the fluted cups,
The obsidian arrowheads, the child's rattle.

I remembered that famous doodle, or riddle,
Five ghosts looking into a pond,
Which I liked to draw in notebooks as a child,
Making the large circle perfect with my compass,
And the half-circles equal in size and distance.
I used to sympathize with those ghosts
Hovering sadly above their lost reflections.
The first year or so after I don't exist,
If I could feel, I'd feel about like this,
I'd think, holding the paper up to light
Which shone evenly through heads and water.

I saw my own head deep inside the glass
Protecting the map, the rocks, the fossils.
The old nun who taught biology
Seemed to be breathing at my elbow then
As if I were back in my girls' school
My hair combed into its stiff wave.
Once she lectured on the mystery of the body,
Moving her pointer over the skeleton
Hanging in the corner of the dark laboratory,
The wings of her white headdress shaking
As she explained the kneecap, and the ribs
Curved to protect the lungs. She made us

Find the floating rib under our blouses
Then told us to look in our emptying bathtubs
For dead cells, those grey and spinning flakes.
We were totally new every seven years,
She said, and we understood by her tone
How the subject was moving finally to religion.

Even then I'd speculate about the brain
Spiraled inside its shell like the conch —
I never saw its cells drifting away,
And yet, whole sections of my life
Seemed to have disappeared in its interior.
I was already bleak and diluted
Like those mysterious and extinct fish
Whose bones reveal nothing of their color.
The father holding his daughter's hand
May have smiled to see me staring at myself
Caught in the wavy glass of the exhibits.
But some night he'd find he was listening
On the edge of her bed, as she described
A dream vanishing as she tried to tell it,
A whole landscape of marsh and greyness
Into which she sank with her arms raised.
I saw I'd drawn a circle in the dust
Powdering the display case, then five curves
Meant to suggest the hollow ghosts
Which the janitor might recognize as he wiped
The glass clean for tomorrow's tourists.
Driving home, again the shining lake
Stretched so clearly under the sun I gasped
Thinking I felt a breeze heard cries of swimmers.

II THE LION'S EYEBROWS

(Meditations on *The Meditations of Marcus Aurelius*)

(I) COMFORT

Somewhere I read that high and low notes
disappear from the human voice on the telephone,
too expensive to send. But I'd pay
for the lost inflection in my mother's call:
She says my father wakes up sweating,
the whole front of his pajamas sopping wet,
and maybe her tone could have told me
don't worry, or isn't this strange?
But she hurries on. I'm afraid to ask why
for it might mean something dark she's avoiding,
the side effects of his new drug,
or the final shape of their marriage.
This far away I forget the ordinary
habits that surround bad news; no doubt
my father, after he swallows his pills for angina,
still reads Marcus Aurelius.
I remember the worn copy
underneath the seat of his armchair,
and the pencil marks below *mildness of temper,*
cheerfulness and *sobriety in all things.*
I think he puts the book down sooner nowadays,
which may mean that he knows it by heart
or even that he's learned to hear
the low moan, rising from the Emperor's lips,
which the black letters sternly hide.

(II) AFTER SUPPER

> "life is a warfare and a stranger's sojourn"
> — Marcus Aurelius

After supper I was reading the *Meditations*,
thinking about my friend's divorce.
Yesterday her quiet letter arrived,
forcing me to imagine
the division of silverware and houseplants,
his boxes piled in the dining room,
and *hers* on the bed they planned to sell.
She relinquished the memory of her husband
all at once, waking to his proffered coffee
and his brown trousers — to a revelation! —
nothing existed but the present.

Later, when I turned off the light,
I thought I heard my parents
quarreling down in the basement
(as if I were a child at home again),
my father threatening to leave forever.
Wasn't that the car door? And now
wouldn't my mother fill the tub
with the hottest water she could bear?
For one moment I lost past and future
like a cloud dissolving into humidity.
How could I love anyone?
If my life was only a *stranger's sojourn*,
then wasn't every day a new hotel
where guests arrived and departed,
saying goodbye with the firmest handshakes?

(III) THE LION'S EYEBROWS

I stamped the dirty snow
caked along the instep of my boot
as I moved down the long corridor
where ugly sounds, almost human,
reverberated through the sour air.
I followed my classmates
past the monkey house and aviary.
I remember the teacher lecturing
before the lions:
"Imitate the old Christians
on their knees and singing,
unafraid of the advancing glare."
One lion, neither gold nor yellow,
dozed on a concrete slab
raising his shaggy eyebrows
at intervals, as if interpreting
her words in some ironic way.
Then the muffled cries of the birds,
the pacing, shaking, the desperate beating
against the firm bars of cages,
roared and roared in my ears —
I was dizzy. I had a cold.
Perhaps I was flushed with fever,
but I seemed to hear my own voice
calling backward from some future
much like the end of a tunnel
echoing with the clamor of gladiators.
That day I saw my life as an arena
and now, closing Marcus Aurelius,
I'll admit the failure of my nerve
for when the lion springs
(even through the vapor of a dream)
I'm terrified of his *peculiar beauty*,
eyebrows, and gaping jaws, and foam.

(IV) TRANQUILLITY

The woman touches the dark wall of her room.
She knows the spiders are at work in the olive tree,
binding together the newest, greenest leaves,
and she offers them a more ambitious task —
to spin the contexture of a web
across the doors and windows of her small house.
She'd like the spiders to enchant her now, now,
at this moment while she lies in her bed
beside her husband who is thoughtfully smoking.
She counts on her fingers all that she will give up.
Her desire for posthumous fame. Her friends asleep
in the suburbs. Even her conversations with her father.
And *gold, ivory, purple, a lyre, a little knife, a flower, a shrub.*
All she wants is a useless and personal miracle.
Now the glow from the cigarette is disappearing.
Of course she knows that it's already later, some other
moment similar to the one before but much sadder.
How long, then, will she press her face into a pillow
murmuring over and over, Dear city of spiders?

(V) AUBADE

"Thou wilt be ashes, or a skeleton,
and either a name or not even a name."
— Marcus Aurelius

Quiet. It's quiet. The blinds pulled,
I could almost imagine the yard shaded
by some iceberg of cloud. Last night
I dreamed of you and that woman.
She was rowing you to an island
where she meant to leave you on the beach
after unbuttoning your shirt, after kissing
those blue veins across your chest,
under the black hair,
which must lead down into your heart.
I suppose she wanted me to find you
with her mouth marked on your flesh —
the way a sea-urchin etches its star
permanently into the limestone.

I'd like to go to her in the future
(a few moments from now, when she'll rise
with her eyes half-shut, her hair tangled)
just to tell her that I'm the one, not you,
who'll always remember her name.
As she reaches for her bathrobe, embarrassed
that I've seen her changed body,
she'll ask sadly, "So there's not the faintest
trace of my kiss?" She'll let the robe fall open.
"Then who remembers anyone?"

(VI) SUBJUNCTIVE

I imagine her mind as a shore, invisible
under the drifts of the lowest sea clouds,
while she stands at the window, her husband
eating at the kitchen table behind her,
steam rising from his bowl of mutton stew.
She's fallen in love with a stranger,
a man walking down her street with a newspaper,
but he *has already passed out of sight.*
She's about to turn back to the yellow room,
her hands aching with all that she has lost.
I observe her silhouette from my own house
across the street, where I lean on my elbows
wishing I were the one who loved the stranger,
who could dream of his handsome eyes.

(VII) EQUANIMITY

> "All things are both familiar
> and short-lived."
> — Marcus Aurelius

It's snowing. The flakes spin.
I've been away so long I hear.
I pay attention. The tiny weights
strike the old snow with a sound
audible only to me when my father,
speaking quietly in front of the window,
pauses in his story about Ireland.
I used to dream about Ireland, he says.
Now I've seen the pasture, the sheep.
I've seen my father's house, the stone wall.
I wouldn't let them pour me whiskey,
but Uncle Tom built a peat fire.
How it rained! I brought cigarettes.

My father's hands open,
then close the temples of his glasses.
I spent two days in Ireland, he says.
I looked out the window at the rain.
That green color. It's heavy.
I wouldn't want to be buried
under grass that green, that heavy.
My father never went back, he says,
and now I know why. It wasn't money.

He leans forward in his chair.
I'm almost afraid to speak
for he looks like my grandfather
who drank tea full of milk
at our kitchen table twenty years ago.
When I take off my own glasses,
the snow seems to fall straight down
across my father's ghostly face.
For once I'm glad I'm nearsighted,
able to stare ahead and see nothing.

(VIII) THE CITADEL

> "the mind which is free
> from passion is a citadel"
> — Marcus Aurelius

I know the rooms by heart, all the places
where the ceiling drops too low
or the floor slants. One stairway leads up,
another winds steeply down into the dungeons
where I swear I heard cries one night
although the cells are empty and well-swept.
Sometimes the chandelier in the great hall
tinkles slightly, its hundred prisms
revolving in the invisible currents of air,
and I've found myself standing underneath
expecting the sharp crystal to fall.
But when I look up, the tiny mirrors
reflect my body back to me in fragments
dispersed into the spectrum of pure light.

(IX) PAS SEUL

> "unity in a manner exists,
> as in the stars."
>   — Marcus Aurelius

Up in the living room, I hear the thud, thud.
My sister is dancing in the basement
where the ceiling is so low she can't leap
unless she bends her head. She knows which pipes
carry cold water across the house, which hot,
for she can stand with her palms
pressed to the galvanized steel for balance.
Now the record's off. She's panting hard.
She's about to come upstairs
with her eyes dazed, her hair dark with sweat.
I used to come up those stairs, too,
into light and noise,
facing my family reluctantly,
some half-finished scene in my hand
describing the sea or the taste of pineapple.

She doesn't see me. She crosses to her room,
dangling her slippers in one hand.
I remember the tale of the twelve princesses
who disappeared down a trap door
underneath their beds each night
where they danced to weariness in a haunted palace.
I never believed they went down together.
I always saw the oldest, in her nightgown,
staring into the dark passage,
her bare heel on the stair, her sisters asleep.
Much later, the others guessed about the lanterns,
the jeweled trees and the shining lake —
but she never told, did not know
how they followed her down at the last.

(X) SMOKE

"look at human things as smoke
and nothing at all"
— Marcus Aurelius

Isn't that smoke across the mountain?
You watch from the study window
while I stand behind you, stroking your arm.
Nothing but singing on the radio, I tell you.
No news. Maybe that's haze up there,
maybe that's atmosphere. You nod your head.
But I know you didn't sleep last night.
Once you touched my hair
so gently I knew what it meant,
having imagined the same hospital,
the same visitor's chair beside the bed.

Ten years ago I woke up confused.
The clouds drift so low, I thought.
How strangely dark on the inside.
Then I remember pushing your shoulder
(you still slept, your hand over your mouth)
and running across the varnished floor.
Through waves of smoke, I finally saw
our landlady burning leaves in the drive.
After I shut the window,
her smoke still rose against the glass.
We could see sparks turning in the air.
Afraid that the roof would catch on fire,
but afraid to abandon our few things
(our typewriter, my wedding shoes)
we sat on the bed in the dimmed room.
I kept looking into your face,
wondering if I'd some day feel this sad
about everything that was going to happen.

(XI) AUDILE

> "after a short time we are all
> laid out dead."
> — Marcus Aurelius

Sunday. Sunday under the olive trees.
A woman walked where everyone walked
looking down at the fallen olives.
As she walked home
she could hear music coming from churches.
Later, when she switched on her radio,
she wished she could play the piano,
just one tune on the piano, even the scales!
And she remembered the late, late movie —
the way the beautiful lady ghost,
unable to rest,
entered the family chapel at midnight
to run her fingers over the organ keyboard,
long draperies flowing around her hands.
At last the rightful heir
turned the key on the mausoleum.
This was a happy ending. Now the woman
feels strangely *vexed or grieved*
as if she misinterpreted the whole story.
She keeps thinking about the lady in the dark
in her stone coffin, forgetting the notes.

(XII) WAVELESS BAY

> "Take away then, when thou choosest,
> thy opinion, and like a mariner, who has
> doubled the promontory, thou wilt find calm,
> everything stable, and a waveless bay."
>
> — Marcus Aurelius

Last night I heard you breathing beside me —
I put my hand over your eyelids
so I could feel the rapid flutter of your dream,
trying to imagine what island,
what waveless bay you'd sailed into without me.
All morning we'd looked at the map of Greece,
tracing our fingers over the evenly tinted sea
from Naxos to Paros to Thira.
Once, when you lifted the map to the window,
I saw the streets of the city on the other side,
visible through the blue water, as if the empty
boulevards and the submerged parks of Atlantis
only waited for us to discover the way down.
In two weeks we'd sail the dotted ferry-route
to Samos, step out onto a shore so fragile
I'd already cut the paper with my thumbnail.
No wonder, as I was approaching sleep myself,
I saw islands the way a bee sees flowers,
illuminated by ultra-violet markings,
each promising its strange but perfect honey.

Sometime later I woke up, coldly afraid.
You were turned from me in some deeper sleep.
It might be months from now, or even years.
Already our trip was over, the map yellow,
the whole Aegean split along its folds.
And though I was still in bed, still going,
I might be remembering some long ago event,
ships I'd sailed in before, shores I'd left.
The future seemed a gleam below the water.
I'd hooked something heavy with my line,
and almost reeled the object to the surface.
Behind me the sailors murmured their opinions,
whether kelp, or mermaid, or rusted anchor,
the bronze torso of a god, or tortoise shell.
I kept pulling the thing up fathom by fathom
all the while staring down into the waves
until I saw, just below the shadow
cast in a black oval by the ship's hull,
a shape I recognized, an eyeless head
emerging slowly from the speculative sea.

III

WILDLIFE CALENDAR

I read my fortune in this calendar
Where animals are frozen into place
Against composed landscape, sky or snow.
In January the shaggy mountain goat
High on his rocky crag meant dizziness
For each day I breathed delusive air,
Dreaming a continent below me,
Strange cities to the east and west.
Now all February, a green sea turtle
Crosses shingle beach above his shadow,
Heading, the caption says, *for the Pacific*.
And marking off the days, I tell myself
He always hears the metrics of the ocean
Above the dull grate of pebble on pebble.

In winter I slowly lift the pages forward
Looking for lucky months. But this March
A long-tailed weasel peers around a log
Alert for the first stir of new-born mice.
The elephant seal's grey and battered head
Dominates April, and at once I know
Why something pulls my eyelid down and down
As if a bit of lead weighted the fold —
When Menelaos wrestled the god Proteus
Through all his transformations, lion and snake,
Leopard, and soaking water and cypress tree,
He hugged at last Proteus' final shape:
A huge seal, rank and sorrowful,
Who croaked the tale of Agamemnon's death.

The whitetail fawn representing May
Stares at her photographer in terror
As if she knows the out-of-focus woods
(Flattened by the telephoto lens
Into the pure green of one dimension)
Will deepen in a moment, glade by glade,
For the passage of her natural enemies.
In June the sober posture of five owls,
Once sacred to Athena, marked with wisdom,
Convinces me that on our literal earth
No libation poured upon the ground
Could draw a goddess down to intervene
In any contest: The owls wait drowsily
For seasonable prey to brave the twilight.

Inside the large square for every month
Each day's a smaller square, and inside that
I might imagine space for hours and minutes,
The minutes filled with tiny second squares
Presided over by the one-celled creatures
Who live inside a drop of water, absorbing
The substance of the water as they swim.
But that perspective makes my room waver:
I focus on the emblem for July,
The curve of antler on the caribou
Against the blue slope of distant glacier,
Finding hope in the grandeur of background,
And in the grasping pose of brown bears
Possibly dancing in the August river.

And now the Eastern brown pelican,
Pressed into abstract shape, his round eye
The center of the pattern he can't see,
Introduces the month of my birthday.
I've seen omens in the visible world
Even since the clown on my pink cake
Caught fire as I blew out the candles
Trying to get my wish. Yet as I trace
My finger over this bird's perfect wing,
I realize I've begun to wish again.
Maybe the habit's deeper than I know,
A permanent spell, part of the autumn
When even the massive cheetah of October
Licks her cubs, her muscles in repose.

Quickly I turn the page to November
Where penguins crowd together on slick rocks —
And now I've reached the end of speculation.
Here the snow falls into the ocean,
Turning to salt; the waves rush up the rocks,
Leave necklaces of foam across the beach
Where the identical birds jostle and slide,
Beginning to form a black calligraphy
In a language I've forgotten how to read.
Stampeding through the December snowstorm
The panting elk see only the blurred trees
Along their nearest way. Not a hoofprint
Exists behind them as they hurry forward
Over the invisible grass of next spring.

THE WILDERNESS

Today the trees are only blazed with paint.
The cannon in Hazel Grove cannot fire
Into the maze of forest which we've entered.
I see the next blue mark, drawing us
Along the lines of the Confederate trenches
Now almost invisible in second growth.
I step past you into a huge web
Spun across the trail. You pull me back.
The colorless threads tremble with our breath.
Later, we see other webs, abandoned,
The shiny bits of wing, the hair-fine legs
Scattered over the sticky bars of filament
Like half-erased words on ruled paper —
Like that page in my childhood diary
I tell you, which I remember rubbing out
Horrified at what I'd written down.
What was it? Only the flecks of something
Cross my brain, now dark, now bright,
Changing the aspect of the woods to bleakness
As if what stalked inside me, stalked outside,
Stirring the twigs, stirring nerves in my neck.
I start to rush ahead through chill air.
The jays scream. Your voice calls me back.

Brushing the gnats from hair and lips, we move
Down the sloping trail across the marsh,
Colder now, and silent. This line of trees
Might stretch across the whole continent
In solid waves of pine and oak, all shadow.
I imagine the two armies in the gloom,
Maneuvering for position, and some boy
Awkward with his rifle, who suddenly knew
He was lost forever in this pathless thicket.
Perhaps I was just now near the fourth dimension,
Standing where his heart beat the fastest.
Now I'm further into the autumn woods
Where he paused, near a trickle of cold brook,
To hug his arms together, renouncing hope.
I think he looked up at the sky, like this,
Then bent to memorize the dead shapes
Of maple leaves, of oak, of red sumac —
Trying to interpose God's perfect details
Between history and his own unready eyes.

SUNDAY GRAVEYARD

"Walks in graveyards
Bore me to death,"
Says the old woman
Walking beside me
Who reads the sunken gravestones
Clucking, clucking —

"Such odd engravings,
A stairway to heaven,
Naked cherubs."
She shakes her head.
Her own stone is smooth,
Pair for, wordless,

"A solid slab
Of grey marble
Thick as a wrist,"
She tells me, pointing —
"No poetry like this."
Just her name

"Elizabeth"
Cut so deep
It won't blur
For two centuries.
"Time enough," she laughs,
"For judgment day."

She calls her husband
Who lags behind us.
She wants her dinner,
Complains of cold.
Half-blinded by cataracts,
She can't read

Fainter inscriptions
Meant to console
Women like herself,
Or warn the ironical
Like me, who think they'll face
Death more honestly.

CHRISTMAS CARD

At times I imagine her face
pressed against my window in loneliness,
or her gentle knock on the door.
Today I thumbtacked my husband's
photographs of spider webs on the ceiling.
I need such a sky to answer her letter.
She only writes at Christmas.
She's afraid of the way her legs swell,
the veins draining blood from her head
as she stands all day at a cash register
unable to think. Last week she saw
her reflection in the window of a bank
& turned her back in embarrassment.
She says she's read of experiments
for injecting sugar into old women
for longer life, & she's worried
her doctor may be lying about its danger.
The sugar in the pith of her bones
dried up when she turned fifty
which explains, she says, her weightlessness,
especially in dreams about skyscrapers
when she floats past her old office
waving goodluck to the typists
with long red nails, still only forty.
When I lift up my blank paper,
its whiteness throws a shadow
across her letter, folded on my desk,
which I've not answered in two hours:
This Christmas I'll send a photo
of a spider web, painting out the fly
until it resembles a perfect snowflake
fallen from the sky above her head.

SHOPLIFTERS

I'd smoke in the freezer
among the hooked beefsides,
wondering about the shoplifters
who wept when the manager's
nephew tugged them to his office.
He made me search the women.
I found twenty cans of tuna fish
under the skirt of a mother whose son
drowned in a flash flood out west.
Now he haunted her,
begging for mouthfuls of fish.
Candles fell from a nun's sleeves.
She meant to light the route
for tobogganists on the convent hill.
Two old sisters emptied beans
from their big apron pockets,
claiming they cured rheumatism.
Soon I recognized snow
drifting across faces at the door,
watching in the round mirrors
the way hands snatched out
unhesitatingly at onions.
In the mirrors everyone stole,
buttoning coats again, looking
once over their shoulders
while eggs bulged in a mitten
or salt sifted from their hems.
Did they think me an angel
when I glided in my white uniform
down the soap aisle, preventing
some clutch of fingers?
An old man I caught last year
stuffing baloney down his trousers
lived alone in a dim bedroom.
The manager said cupcake papers
blew across his floor —
hundreds, yellow, white & pink.
Now he peers through the window,
watching me bag groceries
for hours until my hands sweat.

MAPLE TREE

One day an old man turned his yellow eye
Upon our maple tree, & climbed & climbed
Until his grey coat shook like a squirrel's tail
Above the black hats of the fire brigade
& dancing children, shouting, Fly! Oh, fly!
Wedged in a high crook, his heart bloomed
For the last time; smothered in army blankets
Hand to hand they passed him down the ladder.
Now I remember how his waiting family
Turned, ashamed, to the ambulance,
While neighbors kicked the tree, then, looking up,
Traced their whorled thumbs along the living bark
As if the trunk were braille, & some clear thing
I couldn't understand was growing there.

FATHERS

I

Your father comes to announce
his dissatisfaction with heaven:

He wears only an undershirt
as he stands beside your bed

shifting from foot to foot.
He wants to sleep beside you,

curling his knees
against your wife's back.

After you send him away,
you hear him running water

all night in the bathroom.
How long it takes to shave!

Your own chin feels smooth
against the heat of your palm.

II

Your father is reading
deep in your favorite chair:

You shudder in your pajamas
as you open your razor

showing him the sharp blade
which has cut your chin

so deep that blood
flows in the hollow of your throat.

After he puts you to bed,
you hear him turning pages

all night in the other room.
How long it takes to sleep!

Against your softly beating heart,
your wife dreams of other men.

CHILDHOOD

I used to lie on my back, imagining
A reverse house on the ceiling of my house
Where I could walk around in empty rooms
All by myself. There was no furniture
Up there, only a glass globe in the floor,
And knee-high barriers at every door.
The low silled windows opened on blue air.
Nothing hung in the closet; even the kitchen
Seemed immaculate, a place for thought.
I liked to walk across the swirling plaster
Into the parts of the house I couldn't see.
The hum from the other house, now my ceiling,
Reached me only faintly. I'd look up
To find my brothers watching old cartoons,
Or my mother vacuuming the ugly carpet.
I'd stare amazed at unmade beds, the clutter,
Shoes, half-dressed dolls, the telephone,
Then return dizzily to my perfect floorplan
Where I never spoke or listened to anyone.

I must have turned down the wrong hall,
Or opened a door that locked shut behind me,
For I live on the ceiling now, not the floor.
This is my house, room after empty room.
How do I ever get back to the real house
Where my sisters' spill milk, my father calls,
And I am at the table, eating cereal?
I fill my white rooms with furniture,
Hang curtains over the piercing blue outside.
I lie on my back. I strive to look down.
This ceiling is higher than it used to be,
The floor so far away I can't determine
Which room I'm in, which year, which life.

ALCESTIS

for Stanley Kunitz

She pulled her gown from her shoulders,
kicked off her shoes, then passed a mirror:
Her wan face did not appear.
She left without kissing her husband.

In the boat to hell she discovered
that crowded souls flowed together.
She wept at the casual hands
swarming through her heart, waving

away flies or lighting tiny matches
to view the caverns of dark water.
When she stroked her braid
she could not distinguish it from air.

After the boat docked, she observed
her father on the porch of a hotel
dozing beside the guitar he'd played
at her wedding. She tried to wake him.

Her fingers glided through his jacket.
She could not twang the guitar.
Yet, she thought, a girl once danced
under the stars to its real music.

Would she sleep this soundly? Her father
bowed his head, as if listening:
She sensed the eyes at every window
waiting for her to come inside

where a maid turned down the sheets
on the customary mattress of dirt.
At the door she recalled the candles
flaring on her last birthday cake.

What was it she wished for then?
She glanced back across the river
wishing someone called her name
The stone floor chilled her foot.

The dogs dreaming by the stairs
lifted their muzzles for affection,
but by then she had no gestures left
within her cold and formal hand.

VENUS

> "Bright star, would I were
> steadfast as thou art . . ."
> — Keats

When I saw the evening star
Above sky-shouldering mountains,
I needed my glasses
To focus the pulsing light
Into our closest planet,
A round and diminished world.
For years Venus was hidden
Under its swirl of clouds,
Planet of speculation,
Where giant flowers opened
At night in slow motion,
Each dense, white corolla
Flecked with a thousand gnats.
Then poets could imagine
Shells opening in water,
And round, human arms
Emerging from the darkness —
Aphrodite's hair
Catching on a sprig.

Tonight I know the planet
So brilliant in my view
Shudders under its lightning.
The hot plains of sulphur
Are slowly transmitted to earth
In waves of grey film.
But just as I look away
Toward a sky of smaller lights,
I reverse my perspective:
Seen from another galaxy,
Distorted by light years
And my motion speeded ahead,
I might be only a rock
Hissing into vapor.
Somewhere a dreaming alien
May be shifting a telescope
Disappointed at the blue star,
Even though I'm here,
Standing at the window,
A star caught on my retina
Small as a match flame
And steadfastly falling
Into my brain's gravity.

DIALOGUE

"I feel, that cannot feel, the pain."
— Marvell

I overheard my soul
complain to my body that I slept
uncomfortably in its stiff bones:
"You beat the heart too fast,
twitch her eyelids, pull her muscles
until she turns on the light to read."
Then the body roared, "Oh, no, it's you!
Why did you recall those lovers
she turned away years ago?"
I felt my soul tremble:
"Once she imagined herself water,
moving slowly all day
against the surface tension.
Then you showed her muscles
asserting themselves in her skin."
I turned on my stomach,
knowing I was temporarily solid,
but nervous, as the soul continued,
"You claimed she was opaque.
I see her growing clear,
a pane of glass I could smash.
How will you protect her
from your own changing architecture?"
I wanted the body's lecture
on the nobility of old age,
but I heard only pulse
knocking somewhere in my inner ear.
Then the soul shouted,
"In the desert I'll show you
how sheets of blowing dust
sketch imagines against the sky
of the dead faces
each particle once graced."
My body raged at the soul:

"You'll perish in my mouth —
when the last breath,
drawn up from the lungs,
turns sour as it floats back."
So I sat up in bed
my hand on the light switch.

SONG (AFTER SHAKESPEARE)

When mist advances on the mountain
And Dick the postman shields his mail
And Tom adjusts the furnace fan
   And the cat mews with lowered tail
When the umbrella is our domain
Then softly calls the solemn rain,
                Oh-blue,
All-blue, Oh-blue: a dreary sound,
While lazy Joan creeps back to bed.

When leaves fall on the boulevard
   And quarrels begin among good men
And snails crisscross the sodden yard
   And Marian broods over maps again
When globed drops run down the pane
Then softly calls the solemn rain,
                Oh-blue,
All-blue, Oh-blue: a dreary sound,
While lazy Jack creeps in with Joan.

CAROL

for Greenville, N.C.

Sunday noon. At Evans Tourist Home
No one stares from the metal rockers;
The green paint is chipped
Just where human shoulders rub and fit.

The pine frames of new apartment buildings
Rise from red tobacco fields
As if the whole population
Were building boats in which to sail to God.

Perhaps they've left. Silver bells hang
In celebration from downtown lampposts
Above tinsel snowflakes.
The sky is blue for a thousand miles above.

It looks like the heaven of a storybook
Where the saved walk around barefoot —
And through the Sunday hush
You almost hear the swish of their white hems.

But now the doors of the Baptist Church open.
The residents of Greenville appear
As quickly as a child's fingers
Playing the nursery game Church and Steeple.

Are they surprised to find themselves on earth?
They blink and stutter into talk,
Heading for their cars
Which justify any distance they care to drive.

LITTLE ODE FOR X

Sometimes I call X nostalgia.
My mother telephones her fear of snow
caving the roof in; she hired a man
who rakes it off every time, but today
he's sick & so my mother paces room
after room, watching the ceiling . . .
When she hangs up, I imagine
her face resembling the crisp fly wing
stuck on the storm window, or her raisins
heated in pans until they dry out,
although their bitterness ruins cakes.
Last night a child threw a stone
hard against my front door. That's X, too,
for I've no father to chase him away.
Now I find the stone on the step,
milk crystal so strange I wash
my hands over & over in the kitchen sink,
afraid the child soaked it for hours
in poison from his Christmas chemistry set.
X is the fifth time a friend says no
to dinner, preferring to polish heirloom
silverware until the garland handles gleam,
or my brother's letter from Florida
describing a fight with his third wife.
That feeling of ants in my father's chest,
red fighters circling his heart that night
he sat up in bed, sure of death;
that's X, the specific hum of blood
beating against a clot in my mother's leg.
I hold a mirror behind my own knees,
touching the blue tubes running like roots
into my body, finally an equation for X,
as it, too, now grows by subtraction.

PALINODE

I've saved the milk crystal stone
banged at my door last winter, & the glow-
in-the-dark monster ring from cereal I wear
in bed, so there's always light under the sheet.
On television I see kits that turn
fresh flowers into glass forever, remembering
horseshoe wreaths over a friend's casket
I might have stored behind the armchair.
In a matchbox I've got my cat's grey claws;
when I sprinkle them on linoleum,
she'll bat them idly with her soft, useless paws,
making them click against the stove.
Lately I save everything, even hesitating
over the gnat swimming my beer
or the exploded firecracker from New Year's.
I've tape-recorded my mother's low voice
on the phone, as she describes dahlias ,
or the configurations of her latest X-rays,
her intestines shiny with barium
like felled trees we saw once along a road
in Indiana, tended with caterpillar webs;
although I've lost the cocoon I picked up
at the roadside table where we stopped,
my mother, combing her long hair, looking
curiously at the white, shrouded branches.

ODE TO MOZART

Concerto No. 21 in C Major for
Piano And Orchestra

I — *Allegro maestoso*

I try to listen for the abstract shape
    Of passing music, the gridwork of the tones,
The hourglass arrangement of the chords —
    But the repeating sadness of the piano
Underscores the greyness of the clouds
    Covering the sky I watch, my forehead
        Pressed against a bedroom windowpane
        As I recall an evening
More real than now, when perfect snow
    Fell through the charmed branches of an oak.

The music says I've lost the oak forever.
    I've lost the whitening grass, the small house
Hidden in the blue darkness of the trees.
    I listen breathlessly. Sometimes the notes
Fall dry but green into my careful ear
    The way the acorns drop on piled leaves.
        But suddenly the sound — as if a gust of air
        Blew the straight snow
Weftwise across the black trunks of the woods —
    Blurs into mere background for my brain.

Or background for the sparrows crossing sky
    Edged by the window, their counterpointed flight
Predicted by the continuing melody.
    I see birds flying when I close my eyes,
Already displacing the present with the future
    When I'll feel nostalgia for the haunted hour
        I watched the twilight sky, listening to keys
        Struck by a pianist
Unfreezing Mozart's passion with his hands
    Inside an orchestra hall miles away.

II — *Andante*

I remember my first recital, my curved hands
 Stiffening over the keyboard in the gym
As I listened to the rustle of the parents
 Turning the pink programs in their laps
Looking up my name, the girl on the bench
 Faltering over the simple tune she'd picked.
  I heard the hammers striking metal strings
   As I repeated measures
Over and over, until an anxious hum
 Moved across the lips of my fellow students.

Then in a rush I played the finale,
 Almost fainting as I bowed to applause
Louder than anyone's, meant to cover failure.
 I shook hands in my blue pinafore,
Standing with others behind the punch bowl.
 But there was a funny coldness in my chest
  As I looked up at the ceiling where the sun
   Fell from a skylight
Altered and pale across the folding chairs
 Arranged in a circle around the black piano.

III — *Allegro vivace assai*

I'm only looking in a crystal ball.
    The tiny details of my childhood fade
As if a gypsy breathed away the scene.
    Briskly, the music calls me to itself
Elaborating its high themes to crescendo,
    All personal grief resolving into sound.
        The oak, the house, and Aphrodite's sparrows
            Pulling her chariot
Across the new geographies of earth —
    Captured by the quaver of one perfect note.

I see the lamp behind me, my whole room
    Projected on the dark beyond the sash
And for a moment I imagine Mozart
    Already dead by the age I've nearly reached
Standing beside me, his face in the bleak glass,
    Tapping the first notes of his own requiem.
        He kept composing his necessary music
            Although the winter light
Grew more and more weightless on his eyelids,
    The snow descending for his final view.

IV

TRISTIA

Grant, ye gods, that Caesar make this not my house
and my homestead,
But decree it to be only the inn of my pain.
— Ovid, *Tristia*

I

My old life seems like music after a concert:
The conductor bows, the doors open on traffic.
I'd blame my sadness on another move
Except I've moved before, exchanging birch
For Southern dogwood, dogwood for the sea.
The past appears more spacious, more like a field
Spotted with oak trees where I wish to walk
Than the once inviting country of the future
Where the boundaries are in dispute, the weather
Turning colder by every thermometer.
But I am exiled. No boats ply the ocean
Flowing between me and my native land
Where I grew up restless, inattentive
To the domes and gardens I now long to see.

And yet I may go anywhere I choose
On any road. I think instead of Ovid
Forced to live among barbarians
Who could not read or hear his perfect Latin.
But nothing consoles me this particular night
When every detail of my cold memory
Leaves me breathless under the heavy blankets.
My friends move their lips in pantomime,
The stairs creak like stairs in another house.
My mother might be climbing up to bed.
But all of this is happening under ice.
I feel like Ovid when he saw the sea
Frozen for the first time, the water
Motionless below the slippery shell.
No oar could stir the heavy marble waves
Where ships stood fast;
No curved dolphin could uplift himself
Into the stinging air.

[53]

II

I still descend at night:
I pass through a crevice in ice,
Plunge into shivery water
Toward the unchanging depths
Where schools of fish swim
Ignorant of air,
Never evolving a lung
Or wing or simple eyelid.
Here is the first house.
The porch light shines out
Through sheets of stiff current
While the old roof holds up
Under the press of the waves
As I heave against the door,
My knock soundless as thought.
Then somehow a window opens,
Thrown up by an unseen hand —
I'm inside at last
Trying to touch all I can:
Objects forsaken and rusted,
Toy sewing machine,
Hairbrush, the blue vase
Shaped like a violin,
My cat, curled on the bed
Wanting her back stroked,
Who slides from my wet fingers
As if they gave no pleasure.
Down a wavering hallway
I enter another house.
I pass room after room.
Sometimes the doors are shut,
Or I can't see for mud
Swirling up from the floor.
All my houses are joined
Having sunk to the same place
And overlook the same
Forest of branching coral.

I must prepare for loss.
Already the sea grows murky,
The ice thickens above
Blocking the bright moon.
I only go where I've been,
Open the same closets,
Feel for familiar light cords,
For treacherous ocean sand
Shifts, and swallows up
All the unvisited storerooms.
One year I know I'll find
The ice almost solid,
My fissure a thin crack
From which steam rises
Blinding me when I hover
Above the intimate treasure
Moved away from, or lost.

III

My subdivision grew
Street by street, a labyrinth of curbs
Where unpaved roads
Looped across the cornfields into woods.
Each spring I'd find another dozen frames
Floating on mud like ships under repair.
After the glazier came, I often looked
Into the windows of the empty houses
Wishing I lived in such serene rooms
Without people or chairs or even ghosts
To rustle about with cold, grieving hands —
Unless I counted myself, or counted
A carpenter's footprints in the thin sawdust.
For soon the trucks arrived with rolled sod.
Workmen tamped the shaggy lawns, and spread
Fresh, smoking gravel in the driveways.
Streets were tarred. Moving vans unloaded
Dining room tables, lampshades and toys.

Untidy children stared from the front porches
Eager to tell their names, and learn mine
Until the whole neighborhood was history.
Yet families moved so quickly in those days
That no one planted trees, or only planted
Shadeless plum, and let the nettles wave.

On the Black Sea
Ovid wrote to his friends in elegiacs
Describing the olive tree he planted once
With his own hands.
Never would he see the yellow flowers
Or feel the weight of olives in his palm!
But any year I might turn off a highway
Into a half-familiar town, and drive
Through thinning traffic to that old street
In order to see — there's nothing left to see —
Lilies vanished, the mock orange uprooted.

IV

Midnight chimes. I remember the olive tree
I planted in a place I meant to stay,
A tree unlike the delicate ornamentals
Already in bloom in tubs at the nursery.
I had to dig through layers of caliche
Just to make a passage for its roots
To push down into for a hundred years.
I liked the shadow it cast against the wall
Late afternoons, magnifying itself
As if to show me how it meant to grow.
I hoped to reach, someday on a high branch,
That first shiny olive, small and hard,
And bite into the uncured bitterness.
I used to walk beneath old olive trees
When falling olives stained the sidewalk black
Or blackish red, the color of the heart,
Admiring twisted trunks, no two alike,
Each gnarled into its own private shape
Compelled by weather or a gardener's shears —
And then come home to water my own tree.
Now, tonight, my heart's as far away
From the touch of my hand as that memory,
Impossible either to grasp or forget.

V

Winter after winter in his room
Ovid labored over his careful poems
Meant to rescue him from marshy Tomis.
Then he ceased to watch for arriving ships.
His hair imitated the swan's feathers
As old age bleached him into parchment.
He wasn't always sure what he remembered,
For objects brought up from the sea were strange,
Distorted by ooze, no longer bright . . .

I once thought my own mind an iceberg
Showing only its tip in the smooth sea.
Tonight it seems more like a pane of glass.
That hum I hear, insistent and distracting,
Is only a fly beating his tireless wings
Against the invisible barrier to space.
I try to think of nothing but the air
Entering my lungs, but no trick works —
I'm still awake. I give myself over.

At dawn an ordinary light restores
My few possessions, typewriter and bed.
I'm here by choice — I might be anywhere.
I hear the world, barking and singing again.
This light's exactly like the grave's darkness
Where all of us are equal in our exile,
Ovid no farther from Rome than Augustus.

FIRST MOVE

I ran back and forth through empty rooms
Slamming myself against the blank walls
Where my brother's crib or the radio had stood.
Later, panting for breath, I looked out
All the viewless windows of the apartment
Memorizing the different shades of brick
In nearby buildings until my eyes blurred.
I see myself on the lawn of the new house
Spinning around like a top until the sky
With its perfect blue, its stationary clouds,
Lost its distinction in one swirling shade.
I even recall my next physical act —
Rolling dizzily down the embankment
My mouth involved with sharp bits of grass.
Yet as I rested on the thick, fresh sod
Aware of the speeding earth under my back,
What was I feeling? Exalted or afraid?
The emotion has faded from my brain
Leaving only the movement and the color
So that I cannot guess the reason
That I shiver, roaming this latest house
Where every window lets in the unfamiliar.

BIOGRAPHY

Perhaps biography is the flat map
Abstracted from the globe of someone's life:
We are interested in the routes and detours.
So I found myself last summer in a storm
Driving down the Main Street of Red Cloud
Looking for Willa Cather's house, which was closed.
Then I drove to the Geographic Center
Of the United States, where she may have once walked
When the red grasses covered the prairie.
I tried to see for a moment through her eyes.
I looked at cows; I turned my head away
From the abandoned motel and two roadside tables —
But it was those forlorn shapes I remembered
Back in my own life, out on the highway.

DRIVING THE CORONADO TRAIL

I'm stunned by the high emptiness.
The air is too thin
And yet the road keeps winding up,
Turning among trees
Whose branches are darker than I ever wished.
I see no yellow leaves.

I'm looking for the landscape of a poem
(The first I read in school).
The autumn leaves whirled and whirled
Until a dying child
Who had lost all her happiness in fairyland
Awoke with her heart whole.

When the road twists I see the desert.
The October dust glitters
Against the walls of a copper mine
Cut like a spiral staircase.
On the horizon a thickness of blue air
Imitates the ocean.

If the helmeted Spaniards glanced down
Dizzy from this ridge
They must have longed for their galleons,
Only half-believing
Coronado's tale of a country bright as Castile
And cities of real gold.

As a child I invented such cities,
Watching the cloudy towers
Move along the cold sky of the Midwest.
I meant to travel far
Across the mysterious gridwork of the maps
Reaching my destinations.

Now I'm only looking for autumn
Up on a desert mountain.
The child in my half-forgotten poem,
Let's say she longed to view
The world from the perspective of her future.
She passes into the mist.

Now she's looking through my windshield,
Dreaming herself home.
Where are the hard and the soft maples,
The hand-shaped leaves?
She starts to recite the details of the season
While the black forest presses.

The road climbs through wavering shade.
I see no hectic red,
No thousand shades of gold and vermillion.
When he paused to turn back,
It must have tightened even Coronado's breath,
This chill of evergreen.

AUTUMN IN THE LAND OF THE LOTUS EATERS

Still the season of dark, of reversal.
At noon the sun. At night the cricket
Singing an elegy under the olive tree.
Yet the details confuse us. The grasshopper
Small, brown, and tame, hardly stirs
From his watchful posture in the grass
That roofs the clammy tunnels of the ants
Who file unquestioning into the earth.

And though the oleander blooms, we reach
For the folded blanket as we go to sleep
Hearing a blur of wind, the bare trees
Shaken on the plains of another country —
Such nights we turn and turn in drowsiness
Haunted by the whitening fields of air.

METAPHORS FOR THE HEAT: 101 DEGREES

This heat's so waterless, I think of gold
Some jeweler is stroking across an eggshell
For the King's pleasure. If I close my eyes
I feel the drops of metal on my skin
As the brush smoothes them into a high finish.

So brittle are the mulberry trees today
I hear the spiders moving in their shade
Binding sprig to sprig, and every leaf
Wilts as if a seamstress rolled the edge
Neatly under for her invisible hem.

The glare arrives at my window in waves.
I might be lost inside a diving bell
Somewhere in the deep sea of another planet
Where the molecules of oxygen resemble dust
Mixed into the colorless parts of hydrogen.

The air conditioner seems to haunt each room.
I fall asleep in ghostly shafts of air
Dreaming I'm in a cloud, or standing high
Above the blueness of the bay of Aulis
Just as the Greek ships puff toward Troy

READING FITZGERALD'S *ILIAD*

On the airplane,
I find the page wavering under my glance,
Each word smudged into greyness
So that the blocks of verse
Assemble into the tower of Troy.

Hector has finished speaking to Andromache
Up on that tower,
And merely looks at her, his wife.
I see the hexagons in his eyes,
The perfect tears only a hero can shed.

He has imagined an armed Greek
Pulling the linen dress from her shoulder
Not merely to kiss her throat, but worse,
To hammer the slave's brass hoop
Around her neck until she dies.

I blink the wetness from my eyes,
Forming letters into words, words into lines.
Hector returns to the field
His shield and breastplate heavy with gold.
I watch from the other side of the clouds.

Momentarily I might be Zeus or Athena,
Floating above the earth in my chariot.
But already the plane is banking,
Already descending into a darkening landscape
Toward my small house under sheets of rain.

ATLANTIS

Our new house isn't steady.
I feel water below the floors.
When we sleep, I think it rises
slowly through the cracks.
I'm afraid it's the ocean
for I've found salt on the walls.
When it reaches our windows
we'll cut gills into each other's throats,
just like our neighbors,
then bend our heads into our new element
a mile below the sun.

I think we may carry an umbrella
for the first year
against the immense pressure of waves.
We'll even tap the shells
until tiny air bubbles float out
toward the surface,
which we'll imagine bright with ships.
I'll describe all the clouds I remember,
trying not to notice
how the seaweed tangles in my hair.
We'll dream ourselves on earth.
When you point to the sun,
I'll watch your blurred face,
your eyes closing with disuse.
I won't tell you that the shadow
floating above us is a whale.
I'm turning dark and strange.

VISIBILITY

I have no illusions.
When I roll towards you at dawn,
I can't see you in the fog.
We've simply memorized each other.
I read a story about a giant
who couldn't see his tiny wife
for all the clouds
drifting around his huge, sad head.
He'd stroke the tops of fir trees
thinking he'd found her hair.
In another version, his wife
turned into an egret,
her strong wings
brushing her husband's face;
then she fell into the sea
weighted down by his immense tear.
Let me tell you this:
I miss your shadow, too,
but I know it waits above the fog
black as the shadow of the oak
you saw in your dream
when you woke up, almost happy.
I know our town's invisible.
The pilots on the way to Alaska
think they're over the sea.
Even if they glimpsed a light
through a rift in the clouds
they'd call it a ship
loaded with timber for the south.
Still, I hear those planes.
Last night on the satellite map
I saw a land without clouds.
Remember, I groped for your hand.
Suppose the men go barefoot?
Suppose the women own fans?

RENEWED

As I study our renewal lease
Which reveals a future without snow,
Without palms, without ice or sand,
I think of fairy tales where swans
Turn into stout-hearted brothers
Rescuing their sister from a strange land;
And lean my cheek against the window
Where the glass feels soft but insistent
The way skin feels, over my heart.
Yes, I'm afraid we'll die here,
One of us first, so that the other wakes
Alone at dawn like that last swan in the park,
His wings clipped by a city ordinance
So he can't fly away.
I dreamed we changed into stags,
Our dazzling antlers cracking the ceiling,
Unable to leave by our front door
From where we saw the forest
Bloom, inaccessible, into spring.

OUTLINE

Once I thought this map strange . . .
The shadows of the suburbs fell
pink & blue around yellow city limits.
There I marked X on the main routes away.
Now I'm afraid this city's home.
I've torn the river with clumsy searches
for friends on the other side,
& after taping the wrong bridges together,
still recall their streets, named after
flowers no longer mysterious to touch.
I almost expect to grow old here,
my face stroked into a leaf's design
so unnoticeably that when I look up
at the bathroom mirror, thinking of clouds —
the same way, perhaps, that tiny ant
crossing the map wonders at my huge head
drifting remotely above his journey —
I'll see nothing at all but the glass;
for I've blown the ant off a street
I know well, where old women
sip coffee at the window of a cafe.
As the waitress turns, they steal sugar,
looking neither at me on the street outside
nor at their ghost reflections.

AT THE LANDING

A few days before I die
I'll stand near a river that runs
a thousand miles with no bridge,
thinking back on today, on the greenish
dogwood petals, descending, in the woods
while my husband speaks of a friend
already only a shadow in conversation.
On that future day I'll see clouds
beyond the transparency of my hands
held to the sky's light,
knowing that if I undressed in the street,
children would see each other through my skin.

I feel nostalgia for the old woman
I'm growing into; I'll rise
stiffly from a bench on the long pier
many years from now, recalling the dogwood,
recalling myself, like this, at the window.
Then I'll watch for the ferry
although no friend ever gets off.
I'll have buried them all,
choosing exile in this town
because the streets smell of dying greenery
& once as a girl I dreamed
palms more glamorous than snow.
One day I'll enter the customs shed
with the women who work across the river.
At the rail of the ferry,
as the far shore rises up so blue,
they'll see me touch my heart, sadly,
then fall backwards on the deck,
mistaking their shocked faces for clouds
gathered over my last glimpse of the sun.

ACKNOWLEDGMENTS

Acknowledgment is made to the following publications for poems that originally appeared in them.

The American Poetry Review: "Atlantis," "At the Cochise Tourist Pavilion," "At the Landing," "Dialogue," "Fathers," "The Lion's Eyebrows: Meditations on *The Meditations of Marcus Aurelius*," "Visibility," "Wildlife Calendar"

Atlantic Monthly: "Shoplifters"

Columbia: "Alcestis"

Crazyhorse: "Tristia"

Esquire: "Maple Tree"

G. W. Review: "Driving the Coronado Trail," "Song"

The Iowa Review: "Palinode"

Memphis Review: "Sunday Graveyard"

Moon Pony Press: "Renewed"

The New Yorker: "Little Ode for X"

Poetry: "Biography," "Childhood," "The Wilderness"

Poetry Now: "Carol"